DRONES AND WAR MACHINES

Sneed B. Collard III

R😊urke
Educational Media
rourkeeducationalmedia.com

Scan for Related Titles and
Teacher Resources

© 2014 Rourke Educational Media LLC

All rights reserved. No part of this book may be reproduced or utilized in any form or by any means, electronic or mechanical including photocopying, recording, or by any information storage and retrieval system without permission in writing from the publisher.

www.rourkeeducationalmedia.com

PHOTO CREDITS: Cover photo: U.S. Air Force photo/Staff Sgt. Brian Ferguson, sky © Alexey Repka, radar © argus; Title Page flag © SFerdon; Pages 4/5 © drone U.S. Army photo, map © pavalena, Bin Laden FBI photo; Pages 6/7 main photo courtesy of DARPA, RQ-170 photo © Truthdowser; Page 8 © German Federal Archive; Page 9 © Ben_pcc; Pages 10/11 © US Defense Imagery, TSGT FRANK GARZELNICK, US Air Force; Pages 12/13 photos by Staff Sgt. Brian Ferguson, Technical Sergeant Ben Blocker, US Air Force; Page 14 map © ildogesto; Page 15 © top photo © Bukvoed, bottom photo © aick; Pages 16 courtesy NASA; Page 17 © courtesy U.S. Air Force; Pages 18-21 US Air Force; Pages 22-24 U.S. Navy photos; Page 25 courtesy of Customs and Border Protection photographer Gerald L. Nino; Pages 26/27 main photo © PJF, inset photo U.S. Navy/Northrop Grumman/Kelly Schindler; Pages 28-29 Wright Brothers photo © John T. Daniels, other photos courtesy of U.S. Air Force and U.S. Navy

Edited by Precious McKenzie

Designed and Produced by Blue Door Publishing, FL

Library of Congress Cataloging-in-Publication Data

U.S. Technology Forces: Drones and War Machines / Sneed B. Collard III
  p. cm. -- (Freedom Forces)
   ISBN 978-1-62169-929-3 (hard cover) (alk. paper)
   ISBN 978-1-62169-824-1 (soft cover)
   ISBN 978-1-62717-033-8 (e-book)
 Library of Congress Control Number: 2013938881

Rourke Educational Media
Printed in the United States of America,
North Mankato, Minnesota

rourkeeducationalmedia.com

customerservice@rourkeeducationalmedia.com
PO Box 643328 Vero Beach, Florida 32964

TABLE OF CONTENTS

Ch 1   Silent Observers 5

Ch 2   Unmanned History 8

Ch 3   Why Drones?.............................12

Ch 4   Drone Evolution.........................14

Ch 5   Terrorists Beware 19

Ch 6   Other War Machines 22

Ch 7   The Future of Unmanned War Machines . 26

Timeline....................................28

Show What You Know 30

Glossary 31

Index 32

Websites to Visit 32

About the Author 32

The U.S. Army's MQ-1C Gray Eagle became operational in 2009, and can carry weapons or equipment to disrupt enemy communications.

U.S.A
WARRI

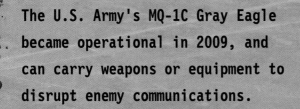

CHINA

Gilgit

Kashmir

Peshawar   ISLAMABAD

Rawalpindi

AFGHANISTAN

Faisalabad

Zhob   Lahore

Multan

Quetta

Bahawalpur

Indus   INDIA

Nok Kundi   PAKISTAN

Sukkur

IRAN

Hyderabad

Ormara

Gwadar   Karachi

Arabian Sea

Osama Bin Laden

4

CHAPTER ONE

SILENT OBSERVERS

On May 1, 2012, U.S. Special Forces swarmed into a three-story compound in northeast Pakistan. Inside the compound lived the world's most wanted **terrorist**, Osama Bin Laden. In 2001, Bin Laden had masterminded the devastating 9/11 attacks on the Pentagon and New York City's World Trade Center. For more than a decade, the United States had hunted Bin Laden. Now, finally, the **Central Intelligence Agency** had located the terrorist. As American soldiers closed in, a powerful new weapon flew silently in the skies above, an aircraft called a **drone**.

Drones go by many names, including unmanned aerial vehicles and remotely piloted aircraft. Basically, they are aircraft that do not have pilots sitting in them. The drone involved in the attack on Osama Bin Laden was an RQ-170 Sentinel. In the months before the attack, the RQ-170 spied on the terrorist's compound, recording movements in and out of it. The night of May 1, 2012, U.S. President Barack Obama probably watched the attack live through an RQ-170 camera. The images made one thing clear: unmanned aircraft are changing the very nature of warfare.

The Navy's X-47B illustrates stealth technology in drones. The plane's materials and wing design deflect and absorb radar signals, making the drone almost impossible to detect.

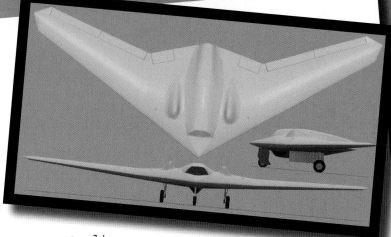

The RQ-170 Sentinel, used to plan and execute the attack on Osama Bin Laden, came equipped with advanced cameras and **stealth** technology that made it difficult for enemy radar to detect.

CHAPTER TWO

UNMANNED HISTORY

Ever since the Wright Brothers flew the first successful airplane, people have tinkered with creating unmanned aircraft. During World War I and II, several nations designed unmanned airplanes. The most famous of these was Germany's V-1 flying bomb during World War II. This primitive aircraft carried a single, 1900-pound (861 kilogram) **explosive**. Simple navigation instruments kept it flying toward its target. Once a counter estimated it had traveled the right distance, the V-1 would simply plunge to earth and explode.

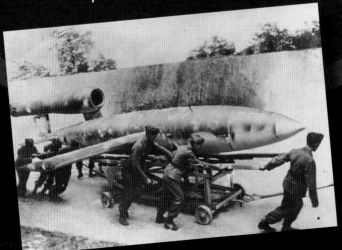

Germany launched about 19,000 V-1s at England and other targets during World War II. Most crashed, were shot down, or missed their targets. Even so, they killed or injured more than 20,000 people in England alone.

The V-1 flying bomb was known as the *Cherry Stone* during its initial development. Later on, it was called the *buzz bomb* or *doodlebug* because of the sound that it made.

During the next several decades, many countries developed more advanced drones. The United States built radio-controlled drones as decoys, training targets, and spy planes. During the Vietnam War, the United States Air Force sent more than 3,400 drones to spy on North Vietnam and surrounding areas. These drones were launched from other aircraft, or used a **catapult** or rail with a rocket to shoot them into the sky.

Ryan Aeronautical pioneered the construction of drones during the 1950s, 1960s, and 1970s, including this Firebee I used for target practice. Some Ryan drones are still in service today.

The Ryan drones used during the Vietnam War had no landing gear. After their missions, they would have to parachute to the ground, skid onto a landing field, or be caught by giant nets.

CHAPTER THREE

WHY DRONES?

But why use drones when perfectly good airplanes and pilots are available? One answer is that the cockpit, life-support systems, and human controls for a modern airplane are incredibly expensive and complicated. Removing these systems from an aircraft saves millions of dollars. Drones have other advantages, too. Because they are lighter, they use less fuel and can stay aloft for much longer, waiting for a target to appear. Drones are also smaller and easier to launch. Most importantly, flying a drone does not put a pilot and crew at risk.

The three-foot (91.44 centimeter) long Raven drone weighs only 4.2 pounds (1.9 kilograms), and can be carried in a backpack. It carries a camera, and is designed to be launched by troops on the ground to observe enemy activities.

A modern MQ-9 Reaper drone costs about $37 million to build. A new F-22 jet fighter costs more than $420 million.

MQ-9 Reaper drone

F-22 jet fighters

CHAPTER FOUR

DRONE EVOLUTION

Despite their advantages, countries were slow to take advantage of drones. That changed when Israel used drones to attack Lebanon and Syria on June 9, 1982. Syria had set up advanced **anti-aircraft missile batteries** in both Lebanon and Syria. Instead of sending their manned attack planes against them, Israel first sent drones. When the missile batteries turned on and started tracking the drones by radar, it told Israeli fighter pilots exactly where the missiles were located. By the end of the battle, Israeli warplanes had blown up 23 missile sites and shot down more than 80 Syrian fighter aircraft.

The Israeli IAI Scout was developed by Israel during the
1970s. It played a key reconnaissance role during the
1982 Lebanon War. It was later replaced by the improved
IAI Searcher.

The IAI Searcher looks almost identical to it's predecessor
the IAI Scout. However, it is well over twice the size of
the Scout. The new design features updated avionics and
sensor systems with greater flight endurance.

The Israelis' success made other countries, especially the United States, pay attention. It's no coincidence that the first modern U.S. military drone was built by a former chief designer for the Israeli Air Force, Abraham Karem. Before Karem, many drones were designed like manned aircraft, but without the crew. Karem came up with totally new ideas for drones and, for the first time, made them extremely reliable. Eventually, his ideas resulted in the MQ-1 Predator.

Abraham Karem built his first major drone, the Albatross, in his garage using a modified go-kart engine. He designed many innovations into the drone. A rear-mounted propeller and an upside-down tail allowed cameras and other equipment to be placed in the nose of the drone.

Albatross drone

The first Predators were designated RQ-1, and were used only for reconnaissance. When weapon systems were added, the Predator became the MQ-1.

MQ-1B Predator:

Speed: 135mph (217.26 kph)

Altitude: Up to 25,000 feet (7,620 meters)

Wingspan: 55 feet (1,676.4 centimeters)

Weight: 1,130 pounds (512 kilograms)

Range: 770 miles (1,239.2 kilometers)

Weapons: 2 AGM-114 Laser-guided Hellfire missiles

Uses: Reconnaissance, Intelligence, Attack

Cost: $20 million

CHAPTER FIVE

TERRORISTS BEWARE

The Predator took drones to a new level. It could fly up to 400 miles (644 kilometers) without refueling and stay in the air for up to 14 hours. It could be packed up in a large coffin-sized box. And it could be controlled by radio or satellite communications from thousands of miles away. During the 1990s, the U.S. Air Force bought more than sixty Predators, and used them to spy on enemies during the war in Kosovo. In the 1990s, the Predator did not yet carry any weapons, but that was about to change.

The 6th Reconnaissance Squadron is an active United States Air Force unit. It is the formal training unit for crews learning to operate the MQ-1 Predator.

Hellfire missiles find their targets with the help of accurate laser guidance systems.

Even before the September 11th, 2001, attacks on the United States, the military and the CIA worried about terrorists such as Osama Bin Laden. They began experimenting with arming the Predator with Hellfire missiles that could attack single targets with great accuracy. The first armed Predator attack occurred in October 2001. Since then, Predators and other armed drones have flown thousands of missions. In Pakistan alone, drones have made more than 350 attacks on terrorists and the Taliban.

The U.S. Air Force is training more drone pilots than fighter and bomber pilots combined, and believes one-third of its planes will be drones ten years from now.

Modern drones can be piloted from military bases and remote locations, including battlefields.

CHAPTER SIX
OTHER WAR MACHINES

Drones are not the only unmanned war machines changing the face of combat. Both **unmanned ground vehicles** (UGVs) and **unmanned underwater vehicles** (UUVs) are taking over many dangerous military operations. Small remote-controlled ground vehicles, or bots, have disposed of thousands of explosive devices in Iraq and Afghanistan, saving many lives. Larger unmanned vehicles have been developed to transport equipment and even to patrol dangerous border and combat areas. UGVs with weapons systems are also being developed.

A U.S. Marine Corps explosive ordnance disposal technician prepares to deploy a device that will detonate a buried improvised explosive device.

The U.S. military already owns and deploys more than 450 UUVs. Their missions include detecting underwater mines, spying on the enemy, detecting submarines, and monitoring ocean conditions. Some UUVs also carry weapons.

A BQM-74E drone launches from the flight deck of the Oliver Hazard Perry-class guided-missile frigate USS Underwood.

The use of unmanned vehicles gives our military a way to conduct warfare more safely, and to find and kill our enemies in places that were once beyond our reach. It also raises important moral and ethical questions. For instance, we are not at war with many of the countries where drone attacks take place. Is it right for us to target and kill terrorists there? Also, even while drones kill our enemies, they also kill hundreds, perhaps thousands, of **innocent** civilians. How can we justify these deaths?

Besides their military use, drones and other unmanned vehicles are also being used by the U.S. Border Patrol, police, and other agencies in law enforcement. Some people worry that these vehicles may invade the privacy of U.S. citizens.

THE FUTURE OF UNMANNED WAR MACHINES

CHAPTER SEVEN

There are no easy answers to the questions surrounding the use of drones. But one thing is certain, unmanned war machines are here to stay. The United States is pouring money into developing more unmanned military vehicles, especially drones. These include large aircraft such as the Navy's X-47B attack jet, as well as tiny drones the size of insects used for spying. More than fifty other countries are also building and using military robots. No one knows the future of these machines, but no one can doubt that they are changing warfare and modern life forever.

Next-generation stealth drones, such as the X-47B, may fly by themselves or in squadrons with piloted aircraft.

TIMELINE

1903:
Wright brothers successfully fly first engine-powered airplane.

1964-1975:
More than 3,400 drones launched during Vietnam War.

1980s:
Abraham Karem pioneers new generation of drones.

1939-1945 (World War II):
Germany successfully uses drones to attack England and its allies.

1982:
Israel uses drones during successful attack to destroy air defenses of Syria and Lebanon.

2001-Present:
U.S. drones used extensively for spying and attacks on terrorists; many new drones and other unmanned vehicles under use and development.

1990s:
The Predator sees major service as spy plane during Balkans War.

CAREERS IN UNMANNED VEHICLES

Unmanned vehicles have spawned a huge variety of career opportunities in the fields of engineering, maintenance, planning, and piloting operations. These careers focus on the military and law enforcement, but are expanding into civilian areas, too. The military offers unmanned vehicle training programs, but so do many colleges and universities. Maybe you will work in one of these high-tech industries!

To learn more about Air Force aviation training, look up http://www.airforce.com/careers/.

For a list of some of the colleges that offer degrees in unmanned vehicles, look up http://www.aviationschoolsonline.com/school-listings/UAV-Training/24.php.

SHOW WHAT YOU KNOW

1. Which countries were the first to use drones?
2. Describe how the military has used drones.
3. What are some of the advantages to using drones?
4. Why are some people against the use of drones?
5. How do you think modern life might be changed because of drones?

GLOSSARY

anti-aircraft missile batteries (an-TEE-air-KRAFT MISS-uhl BAT-uh-reez): units of radar-equipped, defense systems designed to detect and shoot down enemy aircraft

catapult (KAT-uh-puhlt): a hydraulic device that launches airplanes from a ship's deck

Central Intelligence Agency (SEN-truhl in-TEL-uh-junhz AY-juhn-see): an agency devoted to gathering intelligence, spying, and conducting covert operations in order to protect the citizens and interests of the United States

drone (dron): unmanned aircraft

explosive (ek-SPLOH-siv): something that can blow up

innocent (IN-uh-sunht): not guilty and not aware of something

stealth (stelth): in the military, aircraft or other vehicles that are almost invisible to radar

terrorist (TER-ur-ist): a person who uses threats and violence to control or kill people

unmanned ground vehicles (UHN-mand GROUND VEE-uh-kuhlz): remotely operated ground vehicles whose chief jobs are to detect threats and dispose of dangerous bombs and other devices

unmanned underwater vehicles (UHN-mand UHN-dur-waw-tur VEE-uh-kuhlz): remotely operated submersible vehicles whose chief jobs are to detect mines, observe enemy ships and submarines, and monitor underwater conditions

Index

Abraham Karem   16

Albatross   16

Central Intelligence Agency 5

drone(s)   5, 6, 10, 11, 14, 16, 19,
    20, 24, 26

F-22   13

Firebee   10

Hellfire missiles   20

IAI-Scout   15

IAI-Searcher 1   15

Israel   14

Kosovo war   19

MQ-1 Predator   16, 18

MQ-1C Gray Eagle   4

MQ-9 Reaper   13

Osama Bin Laden   5, 6, 7, 20

QF-4   24

Raven   12

RQ-170 Sentinel   6, 7

U.S. Special Forces   5

Unmanned ground vehicles
    (UGVs)   22

Unmanned underwater vehicles
    (UUVs)   22

V-1   8, 9

Vietnam War   10, 11

X-47B   7, 26

Websites to Visit

http://www.airforce.com/

http://www.pbs.org/wgbh/nova/military/rise-of-the-drones.html

http://airandspace.si.edu/education/onlinelearning.cfm?hp=m

About the Author

Sneed B. Collard III has written more than 65 books for young people including the award-winning books *Science Warriors—The Battle Against Invasive Species*, *Pocket Babies and Other Amazing Marsupials*, and The *World Famous Miles City Bucking Horse Sale*. His popular novels include *Dog Sense, Hangman's Gold, and Cartwheel—A Sequel to Double Eagle.* Watch book trailers for Sneed's books on his YouTube channel, and learn more about him at www.sneedbcollardiii.com.

Meet The Author!
www.rem4students.com